ORDINARY PEOPLE

This title was funded by readers and friends via the 2021 VAGABOND PRESS SURVIVAL FUND.

First published 2021 by Vagabond Press
www.vagabondpress.net

Note: Japanese names in this book follow the Japanese convention of family first.

Cover: Rob ZS/shutterstock.com. Image(s) used under license from Shutterstock.com.
Image below: Aniwhite/shutterstock.com. Image(s) used under license from Shutterstock.com.

FUNDED BY OUR READERS

This collection was crowdfunded via the 2021 Vagabond Press Survival Fund.

Thank you to the generous souls who gave big and small. This book would not exist without you.

Visit www.vagabondpress.net for details.

ISBN 978-1-925735-29-1

Tanikawa Shuntarō

ORDINARY PEOPLE

TRANSLATED AND INTRODUCED BY Takako Lento

VAGABOND PRESS

CONTENTS

TRANSLATOR'S NOTE

In his Postscript to *Ordinary People*, Tanikawa Shuntarō writes:

> When I see a café with outdoor tables, I am tempted to sit down and indulge in people-watching. I tend to prefer being alone somewhat absentmindedly to chatting with friends. Those who pass by me are strangers, but I feel an affinity with each one of them as a fellow human, or fellow living creature. I give a name to each one as I please, and often conjure up aspects of the life of each.
>
> I believe poetry, just like novels, is fiction. While novels tell stories, poetry (in my case) simply presents scenes. I want to trust the reader's imagination to weave a story that unfolds before and after a scene.

Poetry has been assumed to be an outpouring of the poet's heart throughout the dozen centuries of poetic tradition in Japan. Yet, during his decades-long career as Japan's most innovative modern poet, Tanikawa has adamantly held that his poetry is fiction. This assertion was ignored or misunderstood by his fellow poets and critics. But he continues to insist on it as a core principle of his poetics. In his postscript to *Minimal* (2002), a book of very short poems which might be seen as haiku-like, he writes:

> I believe what led me to the short form, which had been foreign to me, was my subconscious desire to be silent, and my desire to return to silence to start writing anew. But I am not

sure if I myself have changed, along with the poetic form. Keats said that a poet is a chameleon and the poet's essence is non-self. I will not forget his words until the day I die.

He is indeed a chameleon. During his career, he has been breathtakingly prolific in multiple genres of art. As a poet, he has been innovative, experimental, and philosophical. Each of his books of poetry has been in a different style and theme, and always ahead of its time.

On its surface, *Ordinary People* is a leisurely account of people-watching. These people pass by us, one after another, occasionally remarking on their own circumstances and observations of life. These individuals collectively give us a kaleidoscopic mapping of the world we all live in, even though each is arrested in a moment in life that seems totally mundane or even absurd. But curiously we begin to feel empathy and share with them a thrill of mystery, joy of discovery, or even satisfaction in accepting the enigma of life, as we fill out 'the scenes'. Through this process we watch these individuals, taken collectively, form an intriguingly cohesive universe, just as thousands of miniature photos can create a photo-mosaic portrait. In the end we realize that Tanikawa has forged a picture of humanity in our times, out of a casual parade of 'ordinary' people.

As always, it is a pleasure to translate Tanikawa's poetry. It is thrilling to delve into his poems to see what might be hiding in words, between words and lines … especially since his lines are so perfectly clear and polished on their face. I can never be sure what more is hiding there. It is nonetheless a rewarding experience to explore possible ramifications, even though the effort might help me choose just one word in one line of my translation.

Tanikawa is often playful in his poetry. He teases readers, for example, by saying, 'In every poem, the first person singular lurks.' As a case in point, in 'Mars' a man wonders about the presence of life forms on the planet, an allusion to the title poem in his first collection, *Two*

Billion Light Years of Solitude, where a youth wonders how Martians live. He also embeds oblique tributes to his friends in many of the poems in this book, including [Miyazaki] Hayao, the animation movie pioneer, Chin, the translator of Tanikawa's poetry into Chinese, [Takemitsu] Tōru, the internationally renowned modern composer, [Ikebe] Shin'ichiro, a composer of opera, songs and film music, and Kamei [Katsuichiro], a literary critic and writer. Even T.S. Eliot appears as Tom, with a straight quote of a line translated into Japanese from *Sweeney Agonistes*, and a reference to the cacti in 'The Hollow Men'. But as always, Tanikawa veers off, and makes his own mark. Tom goes back to the 'greenhouse of cacti', not to the dead land, cactus land of 'The Hollow Men'. One wonders if the greenhouse is there to nurture plants, keeping them from the desert, or if it is a subtle reference to the greenhouse phenomenon the world faces now. These people are his associates and friends. They are accomplished artists and are also 'ordinary people', just as Tanikawa himself is.

The book ends with 'Clam Language'. The poem's title made me think of a 1958 made-for-TV movie titled *I Want to Be a Clam*, which was a great hit in Japan in the early days of TV movies. Tanikawa was young and enthusiastic about the new medium. The drama was about an ordinary citizen, reluctantly drafted for the Pacific War. After Japan's defeat, he was tried as a war criminal charged with the murder of an enemy soldier, which he did not commit. As he was awaiting execution, he wrote his last words: 'Should there be a next life, I wish to be a clam at the bottom of the deep sea.' This ordinary man's wish to be a clam is deeply touching. In his next life, he wishes to live in silence, far from an inexplicable world. And in Tanikawa's poem the clam language is a means to open doors to the wider world through translation. The poet hopes to deliver silence, the source and the core of poetry.

Takako Lento, March 2021

ORDINARY PEOPLE

Sumiko
walks through town with a liberated rhythm
she stops as she pleases
she examines the goods on the shelves with care, and
does not buy any of them, which pleases her

Atsushi
picks up the wine list
he crosses his legs under the table
he considers himself unremarkable, and
he receives a gift of a fossilized fern

Yukihiko
picks up a puppy
he throws away a collection of literature
he forgets himself admiring an ancient tree, and
listens for noises

Anri
is comparing this and that
looks into the sky at the railroad crossing
she drinks a glass of lukewarm soda water, and
steps on ants

Ordinary people are attentive
to others who are not like them
lest these feel inferior

which, they are also vaguely aware,
is hypocrisy

Kohji
breeds jellyfish in his bedroom
he sends out gift cards as mid-year greetings
he counts his med tablets
he buys a new pillow

Kimiyo
nonchalantly goes on a short trip
is moved by distant vistas
eats a simple lunch
walks into a stream barefoot

Shin'ichiro
goes to the National Museum
brushes past a princess
a train crosses the steel bridge
birds are perched on a dead tree

Harumi
hates competition
she is watching the sunset glow from the rooftop
holding a bagel in her hand
somewhere in the distance a rainbow appears

Kenzo
buys bet slips at the off-track betting window
he trades jokes with
young city councilors
he watches a re-run of a drama

Mr Anonymous
tirelessly sends in submissions
he buys a book of poems for his daughter
he applies eye drops
he avoids health checkups

Minako
is suspicious of beauty
she blanches leafy vegetables
she looks for Aldebaran in the night sky
she focuses her attention on cervical vertebrae

Amane
unabashedly reminisces
he practices the mandolin
he signs a paper form
he secretly prays

Arisu
makes a bamboo dragonfly
she drinks chai on the terrace
she emails her younger brother
she cries once in a while

Fumio
cannot see the end
Hayao
does not see the end, either
no progress is made in decommissioning the nuclear reactor

Kohtaro
commits a harmless crime

ditto with Osamu
his passport expired yesterday
bees gather around acacia flowers

Chin
thinks he will not die
he writes satirical haiku
he washes his briefs
he sighs

The graveyard for generations of a family and
the graveyard for those with no descendants
sit adjacent to the zoo
people are voluble today, too, but
elephants are reticent

Jojo
believes this is the beginning
he walks out favoring his injured leg
to look for pieces of wood
to hang a small shelf on the wall of his shed

I have
a muscle cramp in my leg
I consult a thesaurus
I eat pickles, and
write this

SCENES

In a scene made of words, not of paintings or photographs
Asakawa sits face to face with a woman
The room is plainly furnished
If the woman opens her mouth, it forces a story to start
Asakawa's silence would be folded into the story

In order to capture a story like a photograph
Plot must be avoided
No name is given to the woman, either
There's a bell flower on the table
Succinct details

A long awkward silence
But a fly is buzzing
One word after another pops up in the woman's mind
But she says nothing
The sun is beginning to set

MY SON

On his seventeenth birthday
My son says
I feel as if I were not born yet

This world is filled
With *Just-So's*
Which cannot be refuted by any logic

Hens keep laying wind eggs in cages
A web of rivers blankets the nation
Emails zip through the air in all directions

A transparent wine glass
His father trusts
His son has no traumas

FULL NAME

I want my full name
The man who (maybe) came from a desert
Is (maybe) saying that to the woman at Window 6
Whatever, that has nothing to do with me
Here I also see an old man using a cane and
A bunch of young women wearing heavy makeup

So-called paperwork is now so important
The forms we mess up while filling them out become wastepaper, but
I hear they get recycled, rather than burned—I feel relieved
But paper money might be replaced by electronic money

Yesterday my client served me *yōkan* from Toraya, which surprised me.

★ *Toraya*: A Japanese confectionary company established in the early sixteenth century, renowned for its *yōkan* (jellied red-bean cake).

ARMS AND LEGS

Poetry now lives only in realities that prose mercifully bestows
This is what Toshihiko thinks, but that's just his idea
Water creates a rhythm as it drips from a faucet, one drop at a time
At the origin of music where words cannot reach
Poetry lurks, even now. This is Mizuhara's view

Somehow my eyes turn naturally to Nature
I regret that I did not say bye on my way out
To the beech tree, older than I am, in my yard
Verbal limbs stretch out like this
In order to use my own arms and legs naturally, rather than words ...

Well, what shall I do   where shall I go?

CANE STORY

Let's talk about a cane, Master says
To do that, we need to jump
From greens in June to snows in November

Master is ninety-seven years and three months old
Day after day he polishes his verse about leaving this world
Bells toll from the nether world

His story starts, here and there, willfully
People appear unrelated to each other and
They even chew on secrets

However many words you use
The Cosmos cannot be dissected alive, says Master
While expounding on the sizes of a whale and an ant

Is a teacup in its original essence when empty?
Or is it so when full?
A Korean folk painting offers a solution, or so I hear

Master left for a walk somewhere
From that somewhere he is leisurely heading to
The third floor of the house numbered 25, so I hear

There are things that remain new
Even after countless repetitions
The best example is morning, as everyone knows

On and on, sweeping in everything in nature
The Cane Story appears to keep going
All the way to the bottom of the Galaxy

A Joseph's coat is swaying in the breeze
Someone is competing with someone else
Sports are the trendy topic

Numerous whispers reach my ears and
Meanings grow increasingly stiff
Who would lament the silence of a teacup?

Master, who tripped and fell, came home
He skinned his knee and magnanimously states
Meaninglessness is meaningful

Giggling and cooing
Children are eating couscous
A pastoral scene on a remote island

Cumulus is a must, says a painter
A sudden fierce squall
Rusted iron scraps on the old battlefield

Numerical formulae fill the blackboard to all corners
Any existence is enduring
Stuttering connotes new learning

The young man who uses a flower's name for his mantra
Has been jailed for three years on false charges
A lizard's-tail blooms by the prison wall

The cane is dozing off again
A crescent moon at mid-day
A fifteen-year-old opens a world atlas

It's been a while since I heard a cow moo
A four-leaf clover
A sudden talk of separation arising in someone's household

The cane, tired of waiting, starts walking
A crazed woman at a kids' bead game
A calico cat chases cockroaches

In a stream smoothly flowing now, too,
Atom, the iron-armed robot boy, is swimming
On a summer evening with swarms of mosquitos over the water

Raising himself from an afternoon nap
Master goes into meditation
Nostalgia in a four-and-a-half *tatami* room

The cane lost its way in the woods
It hasn't chanced upon a suspicious being
Somehow the smell of garlic drifts around

Weapons are scattered all over
Enemies have long turned into sprites
A lone noncommissioned officer is drinking beer

An episode does end at some point
The cane has been lost among the trees and
The first star of evening shines in the planetarium

CONCLUSIONS

To see this morning's sun and recall yesterday morning's sun—
That's a waste of memory
Said a fellow, as if to himself
Which stopped the conversation
Most of our life
Is made up of repetition

The second floor window of the house facing mine
Still has the lights on
Imagination is lewd,
Said Kanzaki once, but he is now senile
I wonder if time actually flows one way

The clock shows 01:08, flicks to 01:09
I am ok with 'i', yours truly, your servant, or the royal 'we'
One evening like this on a Mongolian steppe
I heard wolves howl

Conclusions are always temporary

BOOKSHELF

The bookshelf feels sorrowful
Too many books and it's even impossible to
Separate information from knowledge
Yasuda says he can't wait to retire

Just a finger's touch converts the Roman alphabet into Chinese ideograms—
Which became a matter of course before we knew it
These days prostate cancer is not just professional jargon, you know,
Soeda cuts in,
See, if you keep talking of our times in set phrases
The true value of the Rising Sun and Mount Fuji will decline

So what?
Which might be what everybody is thinking deep down
So I suspect deep down

We cannot soften the bookshelf's sorrows just by reading

MARS

In the cosmos of my heart, day is ending on Mars
Emotions I have never felt before
Silently tell me
There mustn't be any trace of life forms there

The story started quite a while ago and
Will end any day
Words cannot find anywhere to settle down, so
They drift in space, isn't that silly?

Human ears are simply of no use
Audible silence is tangled up with noise
Skin just might come in handy though
Because it could help connect to another's allure

The concept of infinity—How trifling it is!
Delusions of eternity keep spilling out of the world
Voicelessly in secret
Kishi is awestruck by the dusk on Mars

SOLAR ECLIPSE

With Tanaka and Kato and Hanawa here
I learn things I didn't want to know
This is the third time I've sat on the tatami in this party room
A streetcar whizzes by the window
Everybody thinks it's pretty warm for February
Why am I here now?

I bet I drove straight where I should have turned right
Three hot-air balloons float in the sky
There must have been some untold circumstances
Scandals or ugly rumors—are those words already obsolete?
Is everybody late?
Or did I get here too early?

Right about now the Solar Eclipse is starting in Bolivia

ENIGMATIC

Meaning, wearing makeup, trails across the sky
I saw a tiger in an ink drawing walk down the road
Says Yamaguchi
A free-range dream is laying eggs
Like a tangled string
The vista is motionless just like a black and white photograph

Trust me, says Fusako
On a gravel road in autumn in Finland
Back home Iida has been dead for a long time
A kite is flying in the air
About six hours to the national border
Voices are drying into print

And then? He thinks
Dreams come spilling off the cliff
A translation app freezes
Aki'é is toying with bulbs of misunderstanding
The warmth of compost
Germination is not logic

Writing poetry is a product of resignation and
Exquisite linear lines, about three of them, are written
Who was it—the guy who rejected the pleasure of rejecting?
Yoshikawa roars with laughter, sitting straight
The pure white of the enamelware
The red of the traffic signal

Hiroshi is keeping his head down in the library
Someone is trying to write a short story
A homing pigeon is beating its wings
An iceberg is moving forward grindingly
I won't make excuses, says Saeki
Yoko has gone down the stairs with feathery steps

I cannot forget some bars of a certain piece
Of music which I assume I heard in my prior existence
Tōru takes the first train to commute to his seminary
Some cousins machine gears in a small neighborhood factory
In different places of worship all over the world
The words of their prayers are decaying

Nobuko stopped by unannounced
She is chopping onions in the kitchen
The ugly surface of a minor planet is saved as an image
The slender second hand of an expensive wristwatch
The boredom of lost items unable to return to their owners
A radar antenna busily rotates

By the way where is Akiko?
I wonder how she is doing.
On the stage a teapot is sending off steam
While a Pomeranian is scampering around
A middle-aged man with a suicide bomber's belt around his belly
Is washing his hands in the Men's Room

What and to what extent can one make things just with words?
The principled metronome keeps tick-tocking
A ninth-grade girl recites a poem from memory
Daphne is on the shore, in a daze

A single dictionary, digitized,
Slips into Saturn's rings

There's nothing more to write, Chizuko thinks, which
Makes her feel somehow unfulfilled, so again
She begins to write about Li Po
For some reason punctuation is a concern today
In a house where they can see Mount Fuji from the rooftop
Twin sisters used to sing in harmony

Penicillin is a type of mold, says the professor
Pleasant to see cumulus out of the window
An electric bike turns left, unsteadily, at the intersection
At a nursery school Kenji is a popular kid
An aunt snaps the obligatory photo with her smartphone
Of the dish cooked according to a recipe

A spring that's starting to rust is unwinding
Three counterfeit works of art successfully sold at auction
Rica, born yesterday, still has no name
That flag at half-mast, which nation's flag is it?
An ant has lost its way on a chess board
Tadashi, discussing the Constitution, emptied a glass of water

A softball drawn into the baseball mitt
Constellations hiding in the pure blue sky
The toil of reciting the Sutra of the Compassionate Buddha
Which do you prefer, the horizon or the skyline?
Susumu who is meticulously filling out divorce papers
Does not appear on a list of helpers

Who is whispering that leaf veins are secret maps?
As for waffles, I like them plain
The question and answer session ended just a while ago
I make the Ryōanji temple from a plastic building kit
Streams in spring flow with soothing sound
Twenty-four-color crayons are a gift for celebration

The ambiguous life of the Japanese language
Grandmother who does not dispose of a disposable camera
Issei, all his life, walking through the shopping arcade with an alligator
A teacher asks about the meaning of salt on green leaves
A newborn's cute willie
A Watanabe who passed at age 74

Take a good look at it, you'll see
This world is just as enigmatic as the nether world
Says Kim who has been naturalized in Japan
A graph of the life-expectancy of the really old people
A tiger in the ink-drawing is smeared by a sudden shower
The string that was once tied around the scroll has long been untied

PHOTOGRAPH

The one in the middle is Hon'ma
Depressed, he gave up working on his PhD, and
Yearned for an island unclaimed by any nation
So he drifted in his sailboat around the Pacific year round
To his left is Utsuki
The woman he believed was his sister who in fact was his mother
Once he made spring rolls and served them to me
Second from him is Nishida
This fellow saw the world through the eyes of nanotechnology
He was already going bald back then
Tahko is prettier in black and white than she is in person

Hannah took this photo and
She returned to her home country a few days after she discovered
She was in the last stages of cancer
You see in the background
A temple designated as Japan's important cultural property
I recall seeing a news article about it being burnt down, but
I had no particular feelings about that then

Today is Children's Day

LIFE

I wonder how many years it's been since Hozumi passed away
Newspapers magazines TV and radio haven't changed much
Spiders have built webs under the eves
Emperor Taisho is said to be peculiar
An inn where the sound of the waves can be heard
A thick telephone book still remains on the dust-covered shelf

You can write a so-called poem
Out of a list of full names
Ultimately it all depends on how fine the reader's sensibility is, right?
Said the guy in a sarcastic tone

Clouds then clear
I do not want to summarize a man's life
With the word life
This statement can apply to anybody

SORROWS

Although there's no need to say something like this to anybody,
Mitamura opens his mouth, keeping his hat on

Look at the night vista of a big city
In particular, the view from, say, the fortieth floor or so of a building
Red navigation lights flicker on and off here and there
The mountain ridges in the neighboring prefecture are
blurred in the darkness
I don't have to tell you the sorrow in all this.

But sorrows are sorrows
Which are distinct from anything else
Something words simply cannot convey
Just like there is no way of saying pebble but pebble
Neither exclamation nor metaphor,
He says in a calm voice
For some reason chai tasted good that afternoon

Tomorrow, I, Seko
Will visit my mother-in-law at a nursing home

DUSK

He did it on purpose
Purposefully to show it was on purpose
Having heard that, the three fell silent

The so-called depths, I want to know where they are
I want to know how deep they are
Even though curiosity diminishes once you turn seventy-five

I wonder if a group of people can form Arabic letters
Something trivial for Yoshimi might be
A huge issue for his sister in some cases

Who was it said it was fun to answer a question
Requiring a two-hundred-word summary of the meaning of nonsense?
At dusk a man and a woman, waiting for a bus at the bus stop, are
  not in a bad mood

The chimes from the Ward Office sing
A children's song about the sunset's glow

THE UNENLIGHTENED

Graduate students happily discuss the universe but
Their words are all in numerical formulae
So Usami simply lets them brush by
Even if he understood the language, it wouldn't mean anything to him
When will we be able to speak with dolphins?
Brain fog sets in and
He sees three puddles in the empty lot in front of his house
He likes the phrase, 'apart from that'

Day by day he lives as if 'What follows is identical to the previous' so
He dreams of something that emits a flash of enlightenment,
So he writes pages on the computer in the morning
In the evening his wife asks if it is ok to delete it
He can hear his neighbor's TV
Might it be that everyone is burdened with being unenlightened
Since those days when we all looked forward to tomorrow?

A STUDY OF 'THAT'

'That' doesn't care if it is called that
Daphne's fragrance drifts around
A little girl is crying by the roadside, alone
It is that sort of world here

I wonder if a stream ever yearns to be a huge river
People freely use human words and
Ask questions of whomever they please
In Japan, in Thailand, or wherever they bother to travel to

I misplaced what is called a sewing needle
That was one rainy afternoon in the previous century
An old woman came by with unsteady gait
I was not there

He is playing 'Invention' on the toy piano
He is Linus, a Minnesota youth
The drying wash in the backyard flutters in the wind
Soldiers march in unison in a neighboring country

Missiles landed while we were asleep
Rumor has it that dozens of people were killed
Wild chrysanthemums were blooming in the barren field
All these are tales from the past

On the day when I went to see my love
Skipping along the pedestrian crossing

‘That’ was present as always
Nameless, needy, and beautiful?

I peek into the classroom from the hallway
My second son is hiding his face behind a textbook
Commonplace facts are suspicious
The wastebasket is overflowing with waste paper

Sound leaks from the headphones
Vapor trails are breaking up in the wind
I have no object of love or hate
Flowers, centipedes, pistols—I am cool to all of them

No need to separate ‘That’ from ‘That over there’
Once ‘That over there’ changes its shape, it comes close to ‘That’ and
Morphs into something like mountain ridges, says a dreamer
But facts are cold. Ultimately they just converge into nothing

It would be nice if this poem were haiku,
Says a friend, a woman I am not close to
Wouldn’t we wish the words were dragonflies?
Say I, smiling

I rubbed the inkstick on the ink stone to make India ink and
Drew a circle with a brush
In the early morning at four thirty, I went back to sleep
I dreamed of mushrooms growing in a familiar thicket

I cannot get rid of the specter of Mount Fuji
Five students in a Latin class
Even in a country where I hear there is a law to prohibit free association
Same sex marriages are allowed

On the grassy field where a man-powered airplane elegantly crashed
Crickets are chirping
The young man who says he has three mother tongues
Sweats all the time

'That' is indifferent to seasons
Something like a life force that endlessly circulates
Characterizes 'That', but
No one so far has discovered its fundamental truth

A woman says she will express poetry in a picture
I say, please
The resulting picture is so amazingly beautiful
Poetry is holding its breath

I sigh, as I notice it's seven in the evening
With no reason to be sad
A bike with no headlight crashes into a roadside tree, but
No particular thoughts come to me

Thinking of a language which has been lost from the Earth
My cousin, just turned sixty, is crying
Beer and *kakinotane* are on the table
His daughter is sick of news about terrorist attacks

'That' seems to grow silently day after day
Rotating too slowly for the eye to see
It is not clear whether it is moving forward or backward
Because it's ambiguous its coordinates are stable

Somehow or other I went far, but
I don't know how or where I went

I do remember that I walked quite a distance and
That gadflies swarmed all over me

What shall we do with the space between 'Good day' and 'Good bye'
Asks his wife, which sends her husband into a bad mood
Even though it is beautiful, the blue sky is boring needless to say
Just a while ago burnable trash by the roadside was wet in the rain

Just one more time, thinks a boy
Won't be allowed any more, thinks a girl
Someone is searching for their addresses on the web
A story is at its best before it starts

The fan is on, almost soundless
A typhoon is approaching from the south, hot and humid now
Oblivious of the wind and rain a woman is reading Sōseki,
Like a scene from an old Japanese film

His hands dangling from the armrest of his chair
The old man is alive, as if he were dead
The inside of his brain is crowded like an amusement park on a holiday
Is he dead, as if he were alive?

The Japanese language starts with a-i-u-e-o
A child, running down the dirt path by the terraced rice paddies
Calls loudly to a pregnant mom

'That', so precious, is held in her tummy, not in her heart

JAVA SPARROW

Wanting to end it but not able to, that's how this world works
Says Matoba, smiling
Even after death? Says Odagiri
The sinking sun is glaring beyond the cabbage patch

God is in powdered medicine, too? asks Kyoko
She is looking down at the fishing port from the local train window

Hakozaki, at the auspicious age of eighty-eight, tries to extract the world
From the endless numbers of financial data in a newspaper, but
Somehow he cannot recall the surname of
The assistant principal of his grade school

The Java sparrow tweets in a cage
The cat is asleep, totally satisfied with himself
Today is November Fourth.

AURAL IMAGINATION

I am Yakushiji, says Yakushiji
I don't know how many others
Call themselves Yakushiji in Japan, but
I am one of them
My father was a Yakushiji, my son is a Yakushiji, too
Although my daughter is no longer a Yakushiji

The lecture hall has no trace of heating
I wonder if that is my imagination, a duck is quacking somewhere
The Mayor of this town is a Japanese descendant from Brazil

While I am absently listening to the lecture
All at once the face of a love from my past pops into my mind
She had a small mole on her chin

In every poem, the first person singular lurks

GREENHOUSE

Birth, and copulation, and death. That's all, that's all
Tom scribbled that one line with a pen
Rather than typing, and
Went back to the greenhouse of cacti

A neighbor leaves a baby elephant untethered
Grandmother visits him with bananas and such once in a while
Her oldest grandson despises idle fancy, and
Writes a diary every day, listing only facts

A poet's everyday occurrences and those of her grandson—
Where and how are they different?

The birds are now chirping in this neighborhood
The wolf (perhaps) that was howling two nights ago
Lived in the world of LP recordings
The graduate student who recorded it was killed in an accident

Each life form lives in its own way until death

CLAM-LANGUAGE

From the ancient castle on top of the mountain
A girl came down barefoot
She did not belong to anybody
She held common wildflowers in her hand
Kamei sensed something would happen but
A rooster let out a single cry, that was all

Youths in the village were in the library
Studying the local history that was omitted from their text books
The so-called brown sugar incident is missing, too
Rumor has it that the mantra
Which everyone knows, but everyone clams up on
Will be translated into Clam-language and published next summer
How mutable, thinks Kamei
He believes all things are mutable

ACKNOWLEDGMENTS

I would like to thank Mr Tanikawa for granting me permission to translate this book. I thank Michael Brennan of Vagabond Press for encouraging me to complete the translation. I also thank my husband Tom Lento, who supports me as my cultural and linguistic advisor. And as always, I am grateful to all of you, readers and lovers of poetry.

Takako Lento, 2021

About the author and translator

Tanikawa Shuntarō is one of the most widely read and highly regarded of living Japanese poets, both in Japan and abroad, and a frequent subject of speculation regarding the Nobel Prize in Literature. Winner of numerous awards, he has authored over 100 volumes of poetry, light verse, and word-play. In addition he published translations in many genres including the comic strip *Peanuts* and *Mother Goose* rhymes. He has also produced a wide range of children's books, essays, song lyrics, and scripts for radio, TV, and film. He lives in Tokyo.

Takako Lento translates poetry and prose from Japanese to English and vice versa. Her recent books of translation and critical essays include *Tamura Ryūichi, on the Life and Work of a 20th Century Master* (co-ed. Wayne Miller); *The Art of Being Alone: Tanikawa Shuntarō, Poems 1952 – 2009; Collected Haiku of Yosa Buson* (with W.S. Merwin); *Pioneers of Modern Japanese Poetry,* and *Butterfly* by Kashiwagi Mari. She lives in the United States.

www.ingramcontent.com/pod-product-compliance
Lightning Source LLC
LaVergne TN
LVHW030923080826
845145LV00013B/3026

* 9 7 8 1 9 2 5 7 3 5 2 9 1 *